It Is: You Appeared Once

A Story about Potential Dimensions, Abortion, and the Blurry Appearing and Disappearing of Matter

Magdalena Jadwiga Härtelova

s.L.A.p.

sabotage L.A. publishing

It Is: You Appeared Once

A Story about Potential Dimensions, Abortion, and the

Blurry Appearing and Disappearing of Matter

© Magdalena Jadwiga Härtelova 2022

Licensed under Creative Commons BY-NC-SA 4.0

creativecommons.org/licenses/by-nc-sa/4.0

1ˢᵗ edition 2022

ISBN: 978-3-9823344-2-4

s.L.A.p.

sabotage L.A. publishing

www.sabotagelapublishing.com

It Is: You Appeared Once

A Story about Potential Dimensions, Abortion, and the Blurry Appearing and Disappearing of Matter

2022

•

2019

•

2022

•

2022

In the fall of 2018, I became pregnant and about seven weeks later, I had an abortion surgery. In the spring of 2019, I wrote about the transformation that happened, and which continued.

The few weeks after finding out about pregnancy are wild. Like in other moments of my life when I went through a change, when things were dying and being born, this short time was filled with growth and many voices, inside and outside of my head. Why was it difficult to find people who understood that I could be happy with and grateful for the decision to not continue my pregnancy, while still feeling like I have touched motherhood? My life changed by this possibility of a child even though all there was in my belly was a couple of fast multiplying cells.

So came about a story about the short, loving encounter with a parasite inside of me.

2019

The intended line of travel of my story comes to here – part one, Disappearing. I can't say that you are anymore.

•

Is letting go falling?

I will try to speak. But is letting go falling?

I know you understand, but I don't. I have never
touched you. Touched you with my hands, I mean.
You were the expanse of me. My cells your cells.
Cells.

•

Being objective means losing touch with reality.
With cells.

Is letting go falling?

•

I will try to speak in words about the body. The body is called mine. The body is made of stuff. It has physics, capacity, materiality. What happens when stuff leaves my body? At what moment does it stop being me?

I have an immense capacity for expansion, where do I hold all of this? Is letting go falling? And does the capacity of an object – me – mean holding it together? What happens when parts break off? My materiality – me – is just a couple cells.

•

Disappearing. Stuff and cells. At what moment do you stop? Stop being me? Stop disappearing?

Intended line of travel: I will try to speak. I will speak from where I am. I will hide as much as I will reveal. I'm not here, nor there.

•

There is nothing inside of me that wouldn't be me. There is a lot on the surface though: dust, condensation, dead skin, bits of other people's skin from touching me, clothes, nail polish, skin products.

I'm still just trying to speak in words about a body. I know you understand.

You understand. Do you? Understand. That we're moving between outside surface, inner surface. That there are dead parts of what used to be me. That I have an intended line of travel. That I will try to speak in words about a body, that I'm telling a story about having one capable of creating dimensions yet-to-come.

When I'm alone in my body that's when all senses leave me. When I let go, I expect to fall. Sometimes letting go means I fall. Other times it doesn't.

With an immense capacity for expansion, with ripples, voids, and tears, how do I move? How do I let a space exist without trying to fill it?

•

Just a couple of cells, so I assume it's not a big hustle to dispose of it in a hygienic manner. To make you disappear. I woke up and you were gone. I was bleeding again immediately. But you did not disappear. It took my body days to realize it didn't have to grow you anymore.

• •

This is part two, the body of the book, titled Change. Change comes way before the object appears and it doesn't end when you can't touch the thing anymore.

·

Leaving is easy. Letting go is hard. I also know that becoming is touching.

Leaving is easy, letting go is hard. Becoming is touching reality, touching it a little too close for comfort. It's a wild ride.

I know you understand, I wish I would. I know you understand. I wish I would. I have never touched you.

Touched you with my hands, I mean. You were the expanse of me. My cells your cells. Cells.

•

I couldn't keep up the concept of separation between mind and body. But then, nobody said being pregnant is comfortable. It's a wild ride.

With an immense capacity for expansion, with
bacteria, parasites, and multiplying cells, with
ripples, voids, and tears, how do I move? Is the
potential child inside me changing me or am I
changing?

•

I'm used to change. It comes once a month. At least it used to. For the duration of this book, however, I will be suspended above my period, above the bodily changes that loop.

Towards what was I moving? Choosing coming undone instead of becoming whole? Letting go instead of falling, or the other way around? Coming undone versus becoming whole. Becoming undone.

For the duration of this book, I was suspended. When the bleeding stopped, part of my time dimension stopped too.

·

How is falling apart becoming? When things leave my body, when pieces splinter off, are they becoming something else? How? And when? Was something growing in my body or was I expanding?

After all, we are all made of waves – the way that particles appear, then make cells. After all, I'm not flat.

At the end, after, after all, I mean when things fall apart, the space between their particles expands. Cells, cells, waves – constitute everything. When cells splinter off they just create another wave. And waves make up stuff.

After all, we are all made of waves. And waves on water don't cancel each other into a flat line.

•

This is a story about dimensions in potential.

Leaving is easy, letting go is hard. Potentiality is as big as we let it grow. And I was coming to be:
one more person
in a different body
that person
somebody else.

I learned that growing – change – is an exponential function. Mapping exponential growth includes imaginary numbers. And I was coming to be in a different body.

Becoming undone, letting go is hard. Much later, when we talked about the time when I was pregnant, he said potentiality is as big as we let it grow and he didn't let it grow much in his mind. Me? I was coming to be one more person. Expanding beyond what I thought of as myself.

This expansion felt almost alien. You were producing hormones that made me feel like I could do anything, made me afraid of heights, sick in the morning, smell different, feel different.

Leaving is easy, letting go is hard. I learned that growing – change – is an exponential function. Change splinters off infinitely. If I am infinite, if my body can produce other bodies and so on, and so on, where do I end? How do I move? How do I touch myself? How do I hug and comfort myself? It almost felt alien, he said.

•

I felt suspended – suspended above time, in a cocoon of becoming undone.

Being paused means falling into singularity. That's when interpretation fails. When relationships between events are too unlikely for us to comprehend, we have to step out. There is no certainty about the exact duration, about the number of days. We are not smooth and well behaved, our substance is wild.

Stopping to bleed, I was somewhere else. I was becoming to be elsewhere.

What happens when our mind isn't able to interpret something as real – when relationships between events are too unlikely for us to comprehend, when things don't connect, when they don't touch? Substance is what subsists independently of what's the case. I was becoming to be elsewhere, seven and a half weeks in linear time.

•

There is no certainty about the exact duration, about the number of days. But we will call it seven and a half weeks in linear time.

Seven and a half weeks is nothing in a man's life. But I couldn't keep up the concept of separation between mind and body.

Part of me wanted to protect and nurture you, do seven weeks count? But how do I comfort and hug myself? Change is happening, but who is changing whom? Was the potential child inside me changing me, or was I changing?

•

Interlude. There is an obvious question: The pregnancy test wasn't able to detect you until you were about four weeks old. Where were you during that time, before I saw the two stripes? To be clear, I'm speaking from my belly.

I know that I have been a mother. I know that the change has already happened. After all, I felt my hips grow, my breasts grow – they were at least a size bigger. I smelled different. I know I will get an abortion and I'm at peace with it. I'm speaking from my belly.

I have more questions: What is the sound of an asymptote? When faced with two options, is taking all possible? Am I not here nor there, am I the "have been"?

• •

This is part three, the last part, Appearing. That's how I traced my change. I'm showing you through words.

•

Is letting go falling? Falling into... place?

How to let go when your body has started changing already, it has already slipped away?

But what is there to say, the change has already
happened. When the sperm fertilizes the egg, two
bodies merge – two physics, two capacities, two
materialities – they create another dimension.

I had questions: Why did this happen to me? Is
it because I imagined having a child a couple of
times?

Now the change has already happened. Now,
where do I end?

•

I don't believe in miracles. I believed in plurivers-
es. That was quite some time ago.

I have been reminded again that my mind has the capacity to imagine its own expansion. Now what is the meaning of all these waves?

Falling into place. Coming undone, becoming whole. Being made of waves. It's just a couple cells.

Just a couple cells. So I assume it's not a big hustle to dispose of it in a hygienic manner. Once I woke up and I was pregnant, I just didn't know it yet. Once I woke up and you were gone. But you did not disappear. It took my body days to realize it didn't have to grow you anymore.

Even the past is falling into place. Once, I wrote: There isn't anything inside of me that wouldn't be me and it makes me sad, it's just me. Obviously, I didn't think of bacteria.

So what is the meaning of all these waves?

•

I'm trying to show you through words. Making sounds. Appearing. Coming undone, becoming whole.

We were in the state of being possible, intimate yet inaccessible. Now I know you understand. The distance between you and me – the layers of skin and muscles and tissue – just cells – the fact that I can't touch or see you – seems inconsequential. I know you understand, you are me.

.

Sometimes, I dream about you becoming a drone that will forever hover over me. In a good way.

.

There is not much else to say. This is to make a statement that you were here.

Maybe this should have been read from the back to front. Maybe you should have been making sounds. Appearing and disappearing. The blurry lines of falling.

It falls in place. Nothing to be afraid of, my little drone.

Couple cells – with an immense capacity for expansion, with bacteria, parasites, and multiplying cells, with ripples, gaps, and tears.

I know you understand a void as a thing, a space. It has physics, capacities, materialities. If you want, then, it can be described and measured. It could be the meaning of waves. Couple cells. It is: you appeared once.

2022

Once I wrote that objective means losing touch with reality. Looking back now, I feel objective. What I tried to say about my body has become a story.

There were others with me for the ride. I called Ella the moment I saw the two stripes. Alex picked us up from the clinic. Words started coming out – very slowly at first while I was still pregnant and then more formed during the year following the surgery. Marlene, Sharon, Darina, Stella, and many more shared their stories of abortions, pregnancies, and miscarriages as I was making sense of this alien visit. I am grateful that I didn't have to feel alone. A chorus for six voices came out of my writing, and Madelyn gave the recording of this text its own soundscape to live in. Friends and strangers volunteered to embody the text and make it their own. My mom, who would have done very differently than I did, still said yes to being one of the performers when the piece premiered in Prague. I love you. I still don't know what it was like for John to have a potential child, but I know the music he made for it.

I have thought about babies more than once since then.

Some days my eggs feel like stones in my ovaries, weighing down my abdomen. Some days I dream up my chosen family with my friends. It's 2022 and I'm about to become an aunt.

Once, the fact that I chose to have an abortion seemed like a big fact of my life. Have I expanded or have I contracted? Scale is a funny thing.

Now the memories are like the tinnitus that my partner has. It is still a fact of my life but most of the time I don't hear it, its whizzing sound is just one of the sounds of my life.

Scale and sound are a funny thing.

••

About the Author

Magdalena Jadwiga Härtelova is a curator and an artist who works to create training grounds for bravery, autonomy, and liberation.

This book *It Is: You Appeared Once, A Story about Potential Dimensions, Abortion, and the Blurry Appearing and Disappearing of Matter* is an iteration of their text previously titled *Body.(x)^n* that appeared as a sound piece and as a participatory performance. In it, they attempted to hold a layered, at times contradictory, conversation about abortions, one that is still gravely missing, even in countries where the right for abortion is not legally denied.